Five Christmas Plays
with joy inside

David L. Winters

Published by DAVIWIN

Copyright © **2017**
All Rights Reserved
Print: ISBN 978-0-9977747-5-7

Cover: JD&J Design, Inc.
Interior: Gary Jenkins

TABLE OF CONTENTS

1 The Singing Trees

Written by David L. Winters

Cast

Mimsy Watters Wealthy socialite, wife of Harmon Watters, Chair of Meals for Vets

Harmon Watters Wealthy, husband of Mimsy, Avid Golfer

Steven Watters 16-year-old son of Mimsy and Harmon, Basketball Star

Shelly Franklin Neighbor of the Watters, Single Mom, Volunteer at Meals for Vets

Madison Franklin Daughter of Shelly, 16-year-old, Cheerleader

Christmas Tree 1 Live tree from Boy Scout Tree Lot, personality is sassy

Christmas Tree 2 Live tree from Boy Scout Tree Lot, personality is droopy

Christmas Tree 3 Live tree from Boy Scout Tree Lot, personality is hungry

Christmas Tree 4 Live tree from Boy Scout Tree Lot, personality is happy

Scout Master Runs the Boy Scout Christmas Tree Lot

Scene 1

(Setting is the Watters' well-appointed home. Mimsy is putting up a decoration on the dining room table and has a phone up to her ear.)

Mimsy: *(Into the phone)* Yes, I'm still here. Now I need everything to be absolutely perfect. Rack of Lamb with Grand Marnier sauce. Thrice baked potatoes. Asian cranberry salad. Marshall Islands cheese plate. Chocolate meringue pie and cherry cheesecake. That's it. Yes. December 24th. My husband will pick it up at noon. Yes. I know that's Christmas Eve. You close at noon. No problem. I will send him over at 11 a.m.

Harmon: Mimsy, do you have any idea why there is a charge for $2,100 to Macy's on my work credit card?

Mimsy: Just a minute, dear. I am on the phone with Crystal Chandelier Caterers. Everything has to be perfect for Christmas Eve. Okay. He will pay when he picks it up. Goodbye. Thank you.

Harmon: As I was saying … do you know why there is a $2,100 charge to Macy's on my work charge card?

Mimsy: Let's see, honey. $2,100, um, oh yes. That was for the new holiday linens I bought for Christmas.

Harmon: Mimsy, do you realize how much trouble I could get into if I'm caught using the corporate account for personal charges?

Mimsy: Harmon, you are Chief Financial Officer. Milt at the club said you can do anything you want. They are not going to fire you over some trivial matter like this. Besides, it was an accident.

Harmon: An accident?

Mimsy: You accidentally forgot to pay down either of my two credit cards last month. So, I had no money to buy the essentials for Christmas. You know how picky your mother can be when she's visiting.

Harmon: Leave my mother out of this. Anyway, you took my credit card without asking me?

Mimsy: You make it sound like a felony. I'm your wife and I know you wouldn't want me to do without. So, I borrowed your card for just that one purchase and I put it back. You didn't even notice. I figured the company would pay the bill and everyone would be happy.

Harmon: You have got to slow down on the spending. No matter how much I make, it is possible to outspend what I earn. Follow the budget we set up together.

(Mimsy mocks Harmon behind his back as he exits room. Steven enters.)

Steven: Hi Mom, what time is dinner tonight?

Mimsy: Dinner is 6 p.m. sharp. Your father is coming home early, but after dinner the two of us are going to the Kennedy Center for the National Symphony Orchestra Christmas concert.

Steven: When are we going to get our Christmas tree? Christmas Eve is just a few days away.

Mimsy: You and I can go on Saturday morning. What do you want me to buy that will be your gift to your father?

Steven: I don't know. A fancy tie or some golf club?

(Doorbell rings. Mimsy goes to answer it and returns with Madison in tow.)

Mimsy: Steven is right in here.

Madison: Thank you, Mrs. Watters.

Mimsy: You are welcome, Madison.

(Mimsy exits.)

Steven: Thanks for coming over. I am getting so nervous.

Madison: Did you tell them yet?

Steven: Shhh. No. And I don't want to tell them until the moment is just right.

Madison: You know your Mom doesn't like me already. This news isn't going to help.

Steven: That's not true. It is your mother she despises. The two of them work together on that Meals for Veterans charity thing.

Madison: I am pretty sure she throws me in the same bucket with my Mom.

Steven: Don't worry about it. What's going on at your house?

Madison: Actually, that's why I'm here. Mom has to work late at the restaurant tonight and she wants me to go pick out a Christmas tree. They will probably load it for me, but I could use some help getting it out of the car.

Steven: Do you want me to go with you to pick it out?

Madison: That would be great. Come on, let's go.

Scene 2

(Setting is the Boy Scout Christmas tree lot)

Tree 1: No, you don't girl. Do not be crowding my branches. You know I need a little space to breathe.

Tree 2: I can't help it. I'm starting to droop. My branches feel so heavy.

Tree 1: No drooping. There are three more days until Christmas Eve. You got to hold your head up and get ready for that star to adorn your head. We have to be ready for our close up. Christmas is one of the most photographed times of the year. The tree is the decoration centerpiece of the whole thing.

Tree 2: Oh, who are we kidding? No one has picked us out yet and they are not going to pick us. We are the saddest group of trees left on the lot.

Tree 1: What is this "we" thing? I just got here last week on a late truckload from the mountains. I am 100%, Grade A Scotch pine. Look at these branches. It does not get finer than this.

Tree 3: She is such a diva. I need some nutrients. It has been a week since we ate. I am starving to death.

Tree 4: Hey, it rained yesterday. Things are good for us. We are probably going to be the centerpiece of some lucky family's Christmas.

Tree 3:   You are always so positive. How can you stay so happy when I'm so hungry? What is your secret?

Tree 4:   Pine tar.

Tree 3:   Pine nuts?

Tree 4:   Pine tar and I always have a song in my heart. Our Creator made us for a special purpose. All we have to do is stick out our branches, lift our voices and praise the Lord.

Tree 3:   Praise the Lord!

Tree 1:   I'm ready for my solo.

(Music begins. Any Christmas-themed praise song works. Tree 1 should ham it up a bit, as she is the diva.)

(After the song, Madison and Steven enter. Trees remain very still when humans are around.)

Steven: They have several good-looking trees left. I thought they might be all out. We haven't got ours either.

Madison: Yep. They are nice. I love that one over there. *(Stroking the branches of one of the four trees.)*

Steven: What presents are you getting for Christmas this year?

Madison: I've barely thought about it. Mom works so hard at the restaurant. It makes me feel guilty that she gets me anything at all. I'm thankful for the special meal she prepares and I like just being together with my aunt and cousins who come for Christmas dinner.

Steven: It must be tough, since...

Madison: Since Dad passed away. You can say it. Mom has sacrificed so much for me. Thank goodness, they were content to live within their means. We have the smallest house on the block. Mom can afford the payments on her own, so at least we didn't have to move. There is some Bible money guy she follows. She just never over-spends for Christmas or anything. My Aunts and Uncles overdo it on me anyway. They always get me a bunch of clothes and electronic stuff.

Steven: Didn't your Dad have insurance money, when he died, I mean?

Madison: Yes, but Mom saved most of that money for my college. She doesn't want me to get student loan debt. It violates some principle she lives by.

Steven: My parents fight about money all the time.

Madison: That's funny. They probably have more money than anyone in the neighborhood and they still manage to fight about it. I remember when they built that McMansion next door to our dinky little house.

Steven: That was all Mom. She wanted to be close to the city, but in a suburban neighborhood. She couldn't possibly live in just any normal house. So, they bought a rambler and rebuilt it from the ground up. We have five bathrooms. Isn't that crazy, for just the three of us. But the best part is, I got to grow up next to you. You are my best friend.

Madison: Aw shucks, Steven. You are getting sentimental on me and we still have two years until graduation. Are your grandparents coming for Christmas?

Steven: You bet. They come down every year. It's about a 3-hour drive. Grandpa is so nice to me. I love Nana too, but she can be a little hard on Mom. Grandma judges every little thing Mom does. It makes Mom jumpy when she knows they are coming.

Madison: *(Looking at Tree 2)* I think I like this tree the best. What do you think? Do you like it?

Steven: Yep. It is a fine tree indeed, Miss Madison.

Madison: Where's the tree guy?

Scout: So, did you make up your mind?

Madison: Yes. I will take this one.

Scout: That will be $35.

Madison: Here you go.

(Steven starts tying string around Tree 2 as the scene goes dark.)

Scene 3

(Dining Room of the Watters home. Harmon, Mimsy and Steven eating dinner.)

Harmon: This salad is delicious, Mimsy.

Mimsy: Thank you, Harmon. It is a new recipe that I downloaded today from GourmetRecipes.com.

Steven: Mom, Dad, I have something important I need to tell you.

Mimsy: That sounds pretty ominous. What is it, son?

Steven: Well, you know I've been friends with Madison for most of my life, at least since we moved here.

Mimsy: I knew it. What has that heathen done to you? Are you two getting married? You are way too young.

Steven: Mom! I'm sixteen years old.

Harmon: Slow down, Mimsy. Let the boy talk.

Steven: Thanks, Dad. No, it isn't anything romantic. Madison and I are more like brother and sister than anything else. She is my best friend though.

Mimsy: Thank goodness.

Steven: She will make someone a great wife someday, but we don't see each other that way.

Mimsy: Maybe she will.

Steven: What I'm trying to tell you is that I became a Christian at her church. I've accepted Jesus Christ as my savior.

Mimsy: What? I? What are?

Harmon: What your Mom is trying to say is...can you tell us more?

Steven: You know that sometimes I go to Madison's Church for their high school group. Most of the kids are cool and they do a lot of fun activities. Last summer, we went to the amusement park. Just before Thanksgiving, they had a hayride. The prayers and little stories they tell make me feel good inside.

Harmon: Go on.

Steven: Well, last Friday, they showed a movie. In the movie, there was a guy like me and I really identified with the things he was going through ... trying to be good at sports and get ready for college. After the movie ended, the minister asked who wanted to give their life to Jesus. I felt this tugging on my heart and I just knew it was God. So, I prayed to become a believer and now I'm a Christian.

Mimsy: You were always a Christian. We had you baptized as a baby. Your father and I are Christians and that makes you a Christian too.

Steven: Oh Mom. You so don't understand what I'm saying. Yes, you took us to church when we were young. That is your faith. This is a commitment I made to follow Jesus for myself. Anyway, I hope you will come to their church for a special service tonight. We can probably ride with Madison and her Mom. If not, I can direct you.

Mimsy: Well I absolutely will not be caught dead in a church like that. Those people are not like us and I will not stoop to...

Harmon: Hold on a minute, Mimsy. I might go with Steven sometime, just to check out the church and support him in his new faith. Tonight is not good because we already had plans. But I promise you that I will come along the first Sunday in the new year.

Mimsy: I am flabbergasted at both of you.

(Mimsy rises and storms out.)

Harmon: Give your mother some time. She has to process what has happened in your life. It will be alright. I think God is doing something in her will, in her mind. Let's clean up the table.

Scene 4

(Setting is again the Watters' dining room. Tree 1 is standing proudly in a corner facing the audience.)

(Tree 1 sings a solo like Silent Night or O Holy Night)

(Mimsy enters and sets the expensive plates on the table)

Steven: Mom, I have some bad news.

Mimsy: What do you mean?

Steven: I got to Crystal Chandelier Caterers at 12:15. The lights were out and they were closed.

Mimsy: Did you bang on the door? Did you call the emergency number? This is our Christmas dinner. This isn't possible. *(Getting upset.)*

Steven: I knocked, I hollered for help, but the only person in there was someone mopping the floor. He was cleaning staff and said 'everyone gone.'

Mimsy: This is all your father's fault. He knew that he had to be over there by noon. He calls me at 11:30 and told me he couldn't make it due to the traffic. I argued with him for fifteen minutes.

Steven: I'm sorry Mom. If we are all together, isn't that what matters?

Mimsy You obviously have never met your Grandmother.

(Steven exits. Then, Harmon enters from the front door.)

Harmon: Mimsy, I am home. Sorry about the catering. Did Steven pick up the food?

Mimsy: Don't give me your lame excuses. You have ruined Christmas dinner. You had one job...

Harmon: Hold on a minute. You don't even know what's happened.

Mimsy: If you think you can waltz in here and tell some story.

Harmon: *(Sternly.)* Sit down at the table and let me explain.

Mimsy: *(Reluctantly, she sits down.)* I'm listening.

Harmon: The company is being merged with another firm. It will take about a year, but I am going to lose my job.

Mimsy: What? How can that be? You are one of the top guys.

Harmon: I was one of the top guys. The other company has their own CFO and they are taking us over, not vice versa. I suspect that they will want me for a little while to figure out about accounting system, but then, I'm out. We have to get our finances in order and think about the future.

Mimsy: *(Now very serious.)* Will we have to cut back on spending?

Harmon: Wait. Do you smell something funny?

Mimsy: With your story?

Harmon: It smells like a toilet needs to be flushed or something. Pretty stinky.

Mimsy: Oh no. And your mother will be here any minute. She has the nose of a bloodhound.

(Harmon and Mimsy walk to the edge of the stage and sniff. Harmon exits and comes back in a minute.)

Harmon: It's not good. Our basement is flooding. With sewage.

Mimsy: Not today of all days. Well, this Christmas is over, over, over.

Harmon: Sit down, Mimsy. *(She does.)* Mom called after I talked to you. She and Dad slid off the road just after they left their house. No one was seriously hurt, but both of them are pretty shaken up. They turned around and went back home. They aren't coming.

Mimsy: *(Laughs uncontrollably.)* Well, I see. That changes things. No food. No guests. No Christmas.

Harmon: Yes, it does change things. *(Harmon smiles warily at Mimsy.)*

Mimsy: But why were you so late in the first place. You knew this is our Christmas dinner and now we have nothing to serve.

Harmon: Mimsy, I'm losing my job. You can't get up and leave when the whole staff is being told that the company will go through big changes.

Mimsy: Over my misuse of the credit card?

Harmon: No. This isn't about you. We are being bought out. I'm going to go lay down. I just can't talk to you about this now.

(Harmon exits.)

Mimsy: *(Walks over to the Christmas tree and talks to it.)* Some Christmas. Hard as I tried to make this a dream Christmas for everyone, even his choosy mother... I ran all over town buying everyone's gifts for each other. Decorated the house to the nines. This is the thanks I get. Why is life so against me?

(The doorbell rings.)

Mimsy: Let yourself in. *(Doorbell rings again.)* *(Shouts.)* Come in!

(Shelly enters and sits down at the table with Mimsy.)

Shelly: Merry Christmas. I brought you over some homemade nut roll. It's my Mom's recipe.

Mimsy: Very kind of you.

Shelly: Wow. That is one stinky smell you got going on here.

Mimsy: Thanks for noticing.

Shelly: No offense. *(Pauses.)* There is no sense beating around the bush. Madison was talking to Steven and I understand your food is AWOL, your house smells and your in-laws cancelled.

Mimsy: Nothing is private with this family.

Shelly: I came to invite you over to our Christmas dinner. It probably isn't as fancy as you were expecting, but I make a mean ham and the cheesy rice casserole is to die for. We eat in about an hour. Will you come?

Mimsy: Oh, that's very kind, but we simply can't impose...

Shelly: Why do you dislike me so? *(Mimsy shakes her head no.)* There is no reason to deny it. At every meeting for our Veterans charity, you avoid me like the plague. You won't even call on me. The few times I did have something to say, you kept looking at the other side of the room.

Mimsy: That's ridiculous. I have nothing against you. I don't even know you.

Shelly: That is kind of my point. We are next-door neighbors. My daughter and your son are good friends. We should at least have talked over the back fence once in a while. Bad luck isn't contagious. My husband died and that's a shame. I miss him every day, but I decided to go on living. I had to keep going for my daughter's sake. For some reason, God left me here on Earth to do something before it's my turn to go. Why do you avoid me?

Mimsy: Truthfully, I just don't understand you. That's the real issue. How do you stay positive? You work so hard. You have had so much bad luck.

Shelly: First off, I don't think it's luck. God loves me and He loves you. Nothing happens in our lives that God doesn't know about. But even the bad stuff, He finds a way to use it for our good. He loves me. How can I help but to love Him back? I know it would tickle Steven if you came to Christmas Eve Candlelight Service after dinner. You don't have to stay on the outside looking in. God wants you to come into His house and experience Him firsthand.

Mimsy: Maybe I will come to the service tonight. It can't hurt to do it for Steven.

Shelly: That's the spirit. And dinner?

Mimsy: If Harmon and Steven will come, so will I.

Shelly: Merry Christmas, Mimsy.

Mimsy: Merry Christmas, Shelly.

(The two women hug and the lights go down.)

2 I'll Be Late for Christmas

Written by David L. Winters

Cast

Joanie Walsh   Mom, raising her two daughters while her husband in on military deployment

Britany Walsh   Young teen daughter of Joanie

Lily Walsh   Little sister of Britany

Justin Walsh   Husband of Joanie, away on deployment

Maddie   Manager and Waitress at Round-the-World Diner

Fatima   Waitress

Zeke   Wise-cracking short order cook

Cust. 1   Businessman or woman

Cust. 2   Tearful newlywed

Cust. 3   Angel

Scene 1

(Setting is the Round-the-World Diner decorated for Christmas.)

Maddie: Fatima, can you see if Table 4 needs some more coffee?

Fatima: Sure thing boss.

Cust. 1: Thank you. Quick question: will you all be open on Christmas Eve?

Fatima: Yes, until 6 p.m. Then we go home and won't be back until the day after Christmas.

Cust. 1: I'm stuck in town working until the end of the year. It's an audit which has to be wrapped up by the end of the year. Finding food on Christmas Day won't be easy.

Fatima: There are usually a few places open. Check at the Comfort Inn up by the interstate. Their adjacent restaurant may be open

Cust. 1: Thanks, I will check it out. He guzzles down the last of his coffee, leaves his money on the table and hustles out the door.

Fatima: Thank goodness, we don't have to work Christmas. I don't know much about the holiday, but my children are Americanized. They want me home with them.

Zeke: Old man Prentiss is cheap. He doesn't like to pay overtime, thinks it is cheaper to just close than to pay us double wages.

Maddie: Mr. Prentiss cares about his employees. He

wants us to have the time with our families.

Fatima: What do you think about Christmas, Maddie? Is it about Santa Claus or the prophet Jesus?

Maddie: Santa and shopping malls, that's the commercial stuff. It isn't the real meaning of Christmas. Christmas is about Jesus, God's own son.

Fatima: I have a lot of trouble picturing God having a son. How can anything big enough to create the whole world become small enough to father a child with a woman?

Maddie: He didn't actually have a man/woman relationship with the woman, Mary. His Spirit caused her to be with child, though she had not been with any man. It was a miracle.

(Britany enters and hurries up to the cash register.)

Britany: Can someone help me? It's kind of an emergency.

(Fatima rushes over to the cash register.)

Fatima: How may I be of service?

Britany: *(Speaking quickly.)* My Mom called in an order for Walsh. It is probably a bunch of broasted chicken. I don't really want all those calories. She never listens to me. I wanted her to order me a gourmet salad, but you probably only have iceberg lettuce. That lettuce doesn't have any nutrients anyway and I wouldn't get full, so we might as well have the broasted chicken. Is it ready?

Fatima: Zeke, do you have an order up for Walsh?

Zeke: *(Rings the bell. Maddie moves away from the bell holding her ears as if the sound hurt her ears.)* Order up for Walsh!

Fatima: Thank you, Zeke.

(Fatima picks up the order and carries it to the cash register.)

Britany: Thank you so much. I can't tell you how much this means to me. We would be so late for my choir concert tonight if you didn't have this ready. I told my Mom that there wasn't time for us to order food and pick it up and eat it and get to my concert. She said there was time, even though my little sister Lily wasn't even home from her judo class yet.

Fatima: My goodness, young lady. You have a lot of words in there. That will be $32.47

(Lights go dim at the diner.)

Scene 2

(Setting is the Walsh home. Joanie, Brittany and Lily enter and remove their Winter coats.)

Joanie: Your concert was excellent. I really enjoyed seeing and hearing you sing.

Brittany: *(Spoken quickly.)* Do you really think so? Could you hear me okay? Although I don't think you are supposed to hear me. I mean we are supposed to blend together and sound like one big voice.

Joanie: You all blended and sounded like one big, great-sounding voice. Now, hurry off and get ready for bed. I will be in once you get your teeth brushed and get tucked in.

(Brittany exits and Lily walks over to her Mom. Joanie sits down in the comfortable chair and invites Lily onto her lap.)

Joanie: Did you enjoy your sister's concert?

Lily: Yes. It was alright.

Joanie: You have been awfully quiet tonight, Lily. Is anything wrong?

Lily: Mom, do you think Daddy will be home for Christmas?

Joanie: Oh, I don't think so sweetie. He is on deployment and probably–a long way from home. But I know he is thinking about you and wishes he could be home with us.

Lily: How much longer will he be in the Army. One
              of my friends at school said that he is getting
              pretty old for being in the Army.

Joanie: *(Giggling.)* No Lily, he isn't too old for the Army.
              You see, he is so special that the Army keeps
              wanting him to re-enlist.

Lily: Sometimes I wish he wasn't so special.

Joanie: Go get your pajamas on. I will be in there after a
              few minutes.

(The phone rings and Joanie answers it.)

Joanie: Hello...Oh hi Mom...No, I haven't heard from
              him. Frankly, I'm getting a little worried. He has
              never gone this long without calling...Don't say
              anything to the girls when you see them. I don't
              want them to worry...I know God is watching
              over us. It's just, I'm a little tired of being a
              single Mom for six or nine months at a time. He
              always promises me that this is the last hitch,
              but then he re-enlists again. What if he pushed
              his luck one too many times?

(Lights go out in the Walsh home.)

Scene 3

(Setting is the Diner)

Maddie: Can I refill that Diet Coke for you?

Cust. 2: *(Starts sobbing loudly.)* No!

Maddie: Hey. Hey. What's the matter here. *(She gives the woman some napkins.)*

Cust.2: My husband doesn't love me anymore. *(Cries loudly.)* And it's Christmas.

Maddie: Goodness. *(She sits down across from the customer.)* Tell me all about it, sugar.

Zeke: Oh boy! Here it comes.

Cust. 2: I wanted this to be a special Christmas and I bought a set of special plates. *(Sniff. Sniff.)* Our whole family is coming over for the first time. I wanted everything to be special. But, but, but, but…my husband doesn't love me.

Maddie: Does he not like the special plates you bought?

Cust. 2: No, it's not that. He says we can't afford them. He says I have Macy's taste and we have a… Walmart budget! *(Starts sobbing again.)*

Maddie: How long have you been married, honey?

Cust. 2: *(Between sobs.)* Three months.

Zeke: *(Sarcastically.)* That explains a lot.

Maddie: Hush up, Zeke. That does explain a few things. You wanted this to be a special Christmas because it is your first one.

Cust. 2:   Yes.

Maddie: Well sweetie, marriage is a marathon, not a sprint. You have a long way to go and can't get so upset about every little thing along the way. Now it sounds like your guy wants your marriage to last, so he is trying to keep your debts from getting out of control. Now, I'll bet your man has some good points. Tell me something that made you fall in love with him.

Cust. 2:   Let me think a minute. *(Pauses a long time.)* He has dreamy eyes.

Maddie: Okay. That's good. What else?

Cust. 2:   He has big, strong shoulders.

(Zeke hugs a mop and pretends to dance with it.)

Maddie: *(Motions to Zeke to knock it off.)* Well there you go. You don't want to lose a guy like that with dreamy eyes and big shoulders, do you?

Cust. 2:   I couldn't bear it.

Maddie: Let me get your check. While I do, you freshen up your make-up. Then, you hurry home and tell him how much you love him. Reassure him that the plates are a one-time deal and you two will have them to use every Christmas from now on. So that makes them a good bargain.

Cust. 2: I sure will.

(Maddie gets up and brings the check back to Customer 2.)

Maddie: Okay, honey. Here you go. Have a nice Christmas now.

Zeke: I got to hand it to you, you know how to talk to people.

Maddie: That's my job. God showed me a long time ago that this diner is just a front.

Zeke: Like a front for the mafia or something?

Maddie: Goodness no. On the outside, it looks like our business is selling food to people. Truth is that we are here to love people. As we take care of customers, one by one, we are doing God's will. That is why God invented work. So that human beings would take care of each other. The whole money thing confuses the situation sometimes.

Zeke: Feel free to confuse me with a little more of that green stuff anytime. My rent is going up in January.

Maddie: *(Laughing.)* I will pass that suggestion on to the owner.

(Fatima enters and shakes her coat off. She hands two bags of groceries to Zeke.)

Fatima: The grocery was a mad house. I got the last four dozen eggs.

Maddie: Thanks for running to the store for me, Fatima. We will need that stuff for breakfast on the day after Christmas. Can't believe we got so low on eggs, but we have been busy the last couple of days.

Fatima We sure have. These Jesus people sure eat a lot to celebrate his birthday.

Maddie: *(Smiles at Fatima.)* Just two more hours until we close. Watch the tables for me. I need to do a few things in the back room.

(Maddie disappears through the kitchen. Joanie enters and hangs up her coat.)

Fatima: Sit wherever you like. Can I start you with a cup of coffee?

Joanie: Yes. That would be great. One cream and one Splenda please.

Fatima: *(Sets down the coffee.)* Do you need a menu?

Joanie: No. I am just dreading going home. So, I thought I would kill a few minutes here. Do you have any pecan pie?

Fatima: We are fresh out, but can I get you some apple or cherry pie?

Joanie: Cherry sounds good. And a scoop of ice cream. Oh, maybe not. On second thought, just the pie please.

(Fatima writes down the order and goes back toward the kitchen. Customer 3 enters, wearing all white, and sits the table next to Joanie.)

Joanie: *(Into her phone)* Hi Mom. Are the girls behaving for you? I will be home in a few minutes. Justin hasn't called the house by any chance, has he? Okay. Thanks anyway.

(Joanie bows her head and prays silently to herself. When she finishes, Customer 3 talks to her.)

Cust. 3: Is anything the matter, young lady?

Joanie: Oh. Well. Honestly, we were expecting a call from my husband and he hasn't phoned us. I'm a little worried about him.

Cust. 3: Perhaps he has been particularly busy in the office or something.

Joanie: I should have explained. He's in the military. Sometimes he goes out on missions and I don't hear from him for weeks at a time.

Cust. 3: That must be difficult for you. I can relate. I go out on missions myself sometimes.

Joanie: Oh really. What kind of work do you do?

Cust. 3: You might say that I'm a special envoy.

Joanie: Hmm. Interesting. Who do you represent?

Cust. 3: I'm supposed to keep that hush, hush for now. You would know the name if I told you.

Joanie: Very mysterious.

Cust. 3: In my business, I come by all kinds of information. Sometimes, I'm supposed to deliver news to people from my boss.

Joanie: *(Becoming more curious.)* Is it usually good news or bad news?

Cust. 3:   That depends on how the people receive the news. You might say that it is the difference between hope, faith and sight. People may hope for an outcome, even believe that it is going to occur. Sometimes, the actual reality doesn't turn out to be what they were hoping for. It might be better or it might be worse, in the short run.

Joanie: Wow. That is kind of profound, I think. So, you bring news from your boss, but it might be good or bad news. How people respond to the news makes some kind of difference in their lives.

Cust. 3:   You see, the good part about the news I bring is that my boss sent it. This means, he is familiar with your situation and he is going to make whatever happens work out the best for you. Even if it seems like bad news...

Joanie: *(Interrupting.)* So, you are saying that people need to have faith in your boss, even if the news seems to be bad at first.

Cust. 3:   Now, you've caught on. The person I'm visiting today is expecting a call that isn't coming. This person will be disappointed to hear the call isn't coming at all.

Joanie: But somehow, your boss will make everything turn out just right. *(Joanie puts her head down for a minute. When she does, the man in white gets up and slips out of the diner.)* Wait. That sounds just like my situation. *(She looks around for the Customer 3, but he is gone.)*

(Fatima returns with the pie and coffee.)

Fatima: Here you go. Is there anything else?

Joanie: Just one thing. Did you see that guy I was talking to? The one in white?

Fatima: I was in the back making a fresh pot of coffee. I didn't see anyone. Did he bother you?

Joanie: No, nothing like that.

Scene 3

(At the Walsh home.)

Joanie: Okay girls. Grandma and Grandpa will be wait-
             ing for us. Get your shoes and coats on. Let's go.

Britany: Mom, I am really getting worried about Dad. He
             knows our routine every Christmas. Why hasn't
             he called?

Joanie: Britany, try not to worry. He may not call, or
             he may call while we are at Grandma's house.
             We know he loves us. We have to keep having
             faith, even if we don't get the phone call we are
             hoping for.

Britany: Do you sense something has happened to him.

Joanie: Being the wife of a soldier is hard. We have to
             keep hoping and keep the faith. So far, he has
             always come home to us. All the times I got
             wrapped around the axle with fear, it was for
             nothing. Hours or days later, he called. Weeks
             later, he showed up right on time. We just have
             to trust our Father in Heaven for the result.

Lily: Did Daddy call yet?

Britany: No. Get that bag of presents for the Grands.

Lily: *(With excitement.)* Okay. Let's get over there and
             see our presents!

(The doorbell rings.)

Joanie: *(Prays.)* Oh Father. Give me strength.

(Joanie opens the door and Justin is standing there with his duffle-bag.)

Justin: Honey, I'm home for Christmas!

Joanie: Oh, thank God. *(She and the girls mob Justin and hug him.)*

Britany: Dad. I am so happy you are home. Why didn't you call us? You had me scared to death.

Justin: I'm sorry to all of you. My last mission was black ops. I wasn't allowed to tell anyone until I was on the ground in the U.S. again. Then, I thought it would be a neat to surprise you.

Joanie: We will talk about the surprise part later. Right now, my parents are expecting us for dinner. Let's get in the SUV and head over there. You can tell us the rest on the way.

Justin: One more bit of news. Not news you were expecting. The Army is kicking me to the curb. That was my last mission. I'm transferring to the closest base and then I go on terminal leave to look for a job.

Lily: Does this mean you are coming home forever?

Justin: Yes, honey. That's what it means. I'm home forever.

3 Christmas Prayer of Forgiveness

Written by David L. Winters

Cast

Grandpa Marcella's father and Trina's Grandfather

Grandma Marcella's mother and Trina's Grandmother

Marcella Single Mom, Works at eyeglass manufacturing facility

Trina Young girl

Jerome Marcella's husband

Carolers Assorted singers, dressed for caroling

Librarian Works at library and treats Trina kindly

Homeless person Man or woman that Trina befriends

Scene 1

(Scene One opens in the festively decorated home of Grandma and Grandpa. Grandpa is sitting in his favorite chair and reading his paper. Trina bounces into the room, taking off her coat.)

Trina: Grandpa! I'm here. How are you?

Grandpa: *(Folds his newspaper and sets it by his chair.)* Just fine, Trina. How was your last day of school before Christmas vacation?

Trina: It was super, Grandpa. We have to call it winter vacation now. Otherwise someone might get offended.

Grandpa: Oh poppycock. All this liberal progressive stuff is about to run me up the wall.

Trina: Run you up the wall?

Grandpa: Makes me crazy. It is a Christian Country for Pete's sake. Always was. Always will be.

Trina: I am so excited about Christmas. What did you get me?

Grandpa: Oh honey, you know I can't tell you. That would spoil the surprise.

Trina: What if I just sneak over here. *(Walks over to the tree.)* And just take a little look here. *(Picks up a pretty box and shakes it.)*

Grandpa: Then, you would be shaking up Grandma's dental cream I bought her for Christmas.

Trina: *(Giggles. Sets the present down and bounces back over to Grandpa.)* That's silly. No one gives anyone dental cream for Christmas.

Grandpa: Your grandmother and I are peculiar people. Besides, we are smart enough to keep your presents hidden away in the Santa Claus closet until the day of the show.

Trina: It is not a show. It is a gift exchange.

Grandpa: Good point, young lady. And why do we exchange gifts?

Trina: Because God gave us the biggest gift of all in Jesus. We continue the love by giving each other gifts.

Grandpa: Close enough.

(Grandma enters with hot chocolate and cookies.)

Grandma: How about some hot chocolate?

Trina: That looks yummy, grandma. What kind of cookies are those?

Grandma: Those are grandpa's favorite ones: chocolate chip with coconut and walnut.

Grandpa: Now this is a Christmas treat.

(Grandma serves the treats and sits down on the couch with Trina.)

Trina: Grandma, how were things different when you were growing up?

Grandpa: Back in the days when Dinah Shore roamed the Earth...

Grandma: Dear, she doesn't even know who Dinah Shore was. Well Trina, our televisions were black and white. There weren't very many shows on TV, so we spent a lot more time playing outside, making up games and riding our bikes all over town. Around Christmas time, Dad used to take us to a place called Ludlow Falls. They would decorate the waterfalls with pretty lights. We would sip hot cocoa and sing Christmas carols. It was so much fun.

Trina: Grandpa, who was Dinah Shore?

Grandpa: She was a really good singer who became an actress and television personality. I liked her because she was nice and she played golf.

(Grandma stands up.)

Grandma: Trina, I have another pan of cookies in the oven. Do you want to come and help me transfer them from the pan?

Trina: Sure. Grandma. Wait for me. *(Bounces out of the room.)*

(As grandpa tries to go back to his paper, Marcella comes in through the front door.)

Marcella: Hi Dad. How's it going with Trina.

Grandpa: Just fine. She barely got to tell me about her day. You don't have to rush from work to pick her up. We love watching her. How was work today?

Marcella: It was a strange day. My boss called me into

her office. She asked me if I liked working at the company. Of course, I said yes. The truth is that I need my job, more than like it. Anyway, she implied that the company may be having financial problems. She will probably have to let one of the production people go. There are only ten of us and I am second from the last to have been hired.

Grandpa: I see. Do you think you should look for another job?

Marcella: Duh dad. Yes. I definitely will be looking for something else, but that doesn't mean I will be able to find anything. My life is just a mess.

Grandpa: Marcella, you don't need a lecture from me, but I want you to know I am praying for you. God sees everything you've been through. He loves you and he still has a plan, even after all the water under the bridge.

Marcella: Dad, I don't know what I think about God anymore. Since the divorce, I just don't feel his love anymore. If he cared about me, wouldn't God have saved my marriage? Even if God did allow Jerome to divorce me, wouldn't he have caused my husband to pay the child support he rightly owes?

Grandpa: Honey, free will comes into play here. You and Jerome chose to get married. I asked you several times if you were sure about him. After things fell apart between you two, Jerome chose to move to another state and try to avoid his child support payments. That isn't something God wanted, but it is something Jerome chose to do. Your mother and I pray for all three of you every day.

(Grandma and Trina come back into the living room. Trina has her coat on.)

Trina: Momma! Guess what Grandma let me do today?

Marcella: No telling.

Trina: She set up this big old grinder and she let me turn the crank and crush the walnuts for the cookies. Look here, she is sending us some cookies home to our house for later.

Marcella: Your Grandma has been terrorizing adults with that grinder for years.

Grandma: You kids have all your fingers, so obviously I'm pretty careful.

Marcella: Thanks for watching Trina. We have to get home and get our tree put up.

Grandma: Goodbye. *(She hugs Trina and pats Marcella on the back.)*

Grandpa: Goodbye girls. *(He stands up and pats both of them on their shoulders as they leave.)*

(Marcella and Trina exit.)

Grandma: I am a little worried about Marcella. She has a lot on her plate.

Grandpa: We need to spend some extra time in prayer for her and Jerome. I never thought this would happen to our little girl.

Grandma: The world has changed so much from when we started out. Back then, there was pressure to stay together. Now all the pressure is on couples to break up. So many kids fall for the lies out there.

Grandpa: There's a party waiting to happen.

Grandma: All the unmarried people are having more fun.

Grandpa: I married too soon, before the right one came along.

Grandma: Truth is, every mate has their faults. Except you honey. You're perfect.

Grandpa: I know, dear. And I'm modest too. *(He says giggling at his own joke.)*

(Doorbell rings.)

Grandpa: They must have forgotten something.

(Grandma gets up to answer the door.)

Grandma: Jerome?

Jerome: May I come in?

Grandma: Jerome, I'm not sure you should be here.

Grandpa: *(Gets up and comes to the door.)* Jerome, come right on in. We wondered how you were doing. We have been praying for you.

Jerome: Thank you so much.

(They all come in and sit on the couch.)

Grandma: What brings you back to town, Jerome?

Jerome: Honestly, I came back to make things right with my family.

Grandpa: *(With her arms crossed and sounding guarded.)* That's a good start.

Grandma: Those are great words, Jerome. But you know what we mean?

Jerome: A few months ago, something happened to me. God came back into my life. I know that I've done wrong to Marcella and Trina. Somehow, some way, I have to make it up to them. To all of you.

Grandma: You know I watched my baby girl cry her eyes out when you left. Her heart was so broken. Then you refused to pay child support, even at the expense of the relationship with your daughter.

Jerome: I had no job when I first moved out West. Couldn't pay if I wanted to.

Grandpa: Well, you are here now. What are your plans?

Jerome: As soon as I get back on my feet, I plan want to make peace with Marcella and be a father to my daughter.

Grandma: That may be harder than you think. She doesn't want to see you.

Jerome: That's why I'm here. I want to prove myself to you two first. So, you will help me communicate with Marcella?

Grandpa: Eventually. We need to see, as the Bible puts it, fruits that show repentance.

Jerome: For starters, here is $2,000 in back child support. *(Jerome tries to hand them a check.)*

Grandma: Oh Jerome. You can't give that to us. It has to go through the State domestic court system. They won't give you credit unless they get it first.

Jerome: I don't have the address and I don't want to waste half of it on a lawyer.

Grandpa: I will get the address for you. Where are you staying? How can I contact you?

Jerome: I'm at my Dad's house. Call me on my cell phone. Here's the number. *(He hands Grandpa the phone number.)*

Grandma: Alright. You said your peace. Let us think through all this and we will call you when we get the address for you to send the child support payment.

Grandpa: We still love you Jerome, but Marcella was really hurt. Go slow and give it some time. *(Jerome exits and Grandpa sees him out. Then Grandpa comes back and sits with Grandma.)*

Grandma: How can you just let him come in and sit in our living room?

Grandpa: Our hospitality is about us, not him. Would his words have sounded different if I kept him standing on our porch?

Grandma: I don't know, but Marcella is not going to like this one bit.

(The scene goes dark.)

Scene 2

(Same living room. Crumpled wrapping paper is scattered around the room and presents are opened.)

(Carolers are standing outside the house and singing a Christmas carol or two. The family stands at the door and listens to them.)

Grandpa: *(To the carolers.)* Thank you so much. That was beautiful. *(He closes the door as carolers go away singing.)*

Trina: Grandpa! Thank you so much. I love my presents. You and Grandma are the best ever!

Grandpa: *(Hugs Trina.)* You are so welcome, sweetie. I hope you get many hours of fun and enjoyment from them. Grandma gets a lot of the credit because she is the shopper.

Trina: *(Moves over to Grandma.)* Thank you, Grandma.

Grandma: You are welcome, dear. Let's go in the kitchen and you can help me put some of the leftovers in containers for you and your Mother to take home with you.

(Grandma exits and Trina bounces after her. Marcella begins picking up the wrapping paper and putting it into a garbage bag.)

Marcella: Daddy, it was another gigantic Christmas. Thank you so much.

Grandpa: You know we love you and Trina with all our hearts. I wish your brother could have come home from California.

Marcella: Yep. He is so into that little company he started. I sure hope it makes it.

Grandpa: Marcella, I need to tell you something that happened a few days ago.

Marcella: *(Sounding concerned.)* Daddy, what's that?

Grandpa: Jerome came by.

Marcella: What? He's back in town?

Grandpa: Before you get too worried, let me tell you what he said. *(Marcella sits down.)* Your mother and I were very surprised to see him. He just showed up on our doorstep.

Marcella: *(Sounding bitter.)* That sounds like Jerome.

Grandpa: He asked to speak to us because he knows that he is not allowed to speak to you or Trina. His main point was that he knows he made a mistake.

Marcella: Stop right there. If he thinks he is going to wheedle his way back into our lives with hat in hand...

Grandpa: Listen to the rest of the story. He seemed quite sincere. He has saved $2,000 toward the unpaid child support. He wanted to hand me a check, but I insisted he send it through the State office, which he agreed to do. Jerome realizes that he needs actions, not words. His primary concern is doing right by Trina first and then the rest of us, he said.

Marcella: All I'm going to say is…we'll see. Promises are one thing, but proven character is something else.

Grandpa: I agree. We are believers, Marcella. It doesn't mean we have to be gullible, but it also precludes us from being hard-hearted. That's one of the messages of Christmas, fresh hope for a weary world.

Marcella: Dad, I've been hurt. Not superficially. I am hurt down to my core. The man who said he wanted to spend his life with me just left me in an instant. Now, he's back and saying all the right things. I need time.

Grandpa: And you shall have it. All you need to do right now is be open to God paving the way for forgiveness. It may take substantial time, but for Trina's sake and for your own, give forgiveness a chance.

Marcella: It is all I can do. Merry Christmas, Dad.

Grandpa: Merry Christmas.

Scene 3

(Takes place at the library)

Trina: *(After setting her books on the returns desk.)* Momma, what shall I read next? We still have another week off school and I don't want to read more Christmas books.

Marcella: Well, let's look over here. There were some mysteries that looked interesting. Let's see if they have a series that you could begin. *(They browse the books and select a couple.)*

Librarian: *(To homeless person.)* Hon, you are going to have to move along. You've been in her over the three-hour limit.

H. Person: Just a few more minutes, Miss Librarian. It's cold out there and I don't have any place to go today.

Librarian: Fifteen more minutes and then I want you out for the rest of the day. Don't make me call security.

H. Person: Alright. I will just go back out in cold. *(Shakes head and mutters to self.)*

Trina: *(Walks over to Homeless Person.)* Hi. My name's Trina. What's yours?

H. Person: I don't have no name little girl. Just a street person, that's all.

Trina: Has anyone told you that you have nice eyes?

H. Person: Not in a long, long time.

Marcella: *(Sees what Trina is doing and walks over to join them.)* I see you met my daughter.

H. Person: She is a fine young lady. Must have a great mother. Wish mine would have been like you. Mama was fond of the bottle.

Marcella: Sorry to hear that. Our Church feeds the homeless lunch on Wednesdays. If you hurry over there, you can get a meal. Here's a bulletin with the church's address. Less than a ten-minute walk.

H. Person: Thank you. Do you have a couple of bucks you can spare?

Marcella: Normally, no. But I just got a few unexpected dollars, so here's two. Don't spend them on anything bad. You are loved, you know. God loves you.

H. Person: Thank you. Bless you. *(Hurries off.)*

Trina: Mama, how does someone get like that? It scares me that we might be homeless someday.

Marcella: Honey. There is a saying, except for the grace of God, there go I. It means that without God, we all could be in that place.

Trina: So if I follow God's way, I won't be homeless?

Marcella: Probably not. You have a lot on the ball. If you keep working hard and praying over your decisions, He will show you the way. We just have to keep showing love to everyone.

Trina: Mama, why can you show love to everyone, even that homeless guy, but not to my Daddy?

Marcella: *(Pauses.)* Oh Trina. Grownups act funny when they get hurt. Your Daddy hurt my feelings by running away from us. I just need some time to get over it.

Trina: I still love him. He's my Dad.

Marcella: I know sweetie. I have a big surprise for you. Didn't want to tell you until it was official. Your Dad has started paying the child support he owes. If he keeps it up, you will get to see him again soon.

Trina: Oh mama. That is the best Christmas present of all.

4 The Christmas Cabin

Written by David L. Winters

Cast

Beverly Mother of Brenda and Shonda, Stay-at-home Mom and now part-time real estate agent

Brenda Accountant for a large corporation

Shonda Office manager for a medical practice

Marcie Artsy type, painter and sculptor

Bill Corporate executive, wears designer sweaters

Wendell Old codger who seems very much at home in the outdoors.

Scene 1

(Setting: Interior of the cabin. Drop clothes over the couch and chair. Fireplace cold and dark.)

(Beverly, Brenda and Shonda enter with their overnight bags and brush snow off their coats before hanging them up.)

Beverly: Come on in girls. We made it.

Brenda: That was so much fun. I forgot what a good time my Mom and sister can be.

Shonda: I feel the same way. Not sure when I've had more fun with an accountant and my Mom. That lunch was stupendous. How about that gorgeous mountain inn?

Brenda: And bistro. *(All three of them laugh at this.)* Thanks for remembering I'm an accountant.

Shonda: That waiter was so uptight. He wanted to make sure we knew it was a bistro too. Not just some restaurant at an inn.

Beverly: Bistro waiters get larger tips than inn waiters apparently. *(They all chuckle again.)*

Brenda: I will go grab the groceries out of the car.

Shonda: And the wine before it freezes.

Beverly: Oh honey, I didn't bring any wine. There are some things I wanted to talk about with you girls and Bill.

Shonda: No wine? *(Makes disappointed look.)* Wine makes talking go better.

Beverly: Not this time. Sorry honey. We want to go over our estate plan. And no, we aren't dying soon.

(Brenda and Shonda head out to the car to retrieve several grocery bags of food.)

Brenda: This seems like a lot for just tomorrow and breakfast on Sunday.

Beverly: It's the strangest thing. I felt like the Holy Spirit kept telling me to keep buying stuff. Who knows?

Shonda: Maybe we'll get snowed in and be here for a month!

Brenda: That's a thought. Not a good one, but that's a thought.

Shonda: Wouldn't it be fun to be together for a whole month. How could our bosses object? Even the doctors where I work. They will just have to schedule their own patients.

Brenda: My job doesn't care how much I'm away from the office, but they expect the work to get done anyway. Payroll waits for no woman.

Beverly: Same with real estate. I have to be available for my clients.

Shonda: A month without wine and I might not survive anyway.

Beverly: You worry me sometimes, Shonda.

Shonda: I love you, Mom. *(Hugs Beverly.)* Working in the hotel business, wine is just a fixture in our world.

Brenda: The snow is really coming down out there. I hope Dad can make it up the mountain.

Beverly: Don't worry about Bill. If he's determined, he can do anything. I'm sure he doesn't want to miss Christmas with his daughters.

Shonda: Brenda, help me get the lights on the tree. *(Brenda crosses to assist Shonda.)* This old tree is getting beaten down with the years. Remember when we got these nautical ornaments. I still love this little sailboat.

Brenda: That was a great vacation. Every Christmas, we can re-live the fun vacation memories with the ornaments. That one is from the Wisconsin Dells. Dad was smart to buy this cabin. It has so many memories of just our family.

(There is a knock at the door. Beverly crosses to the door and pauses before she opens it.)

Beverly: That's odd. Bill never knocks before he comes in. *(Opens door.)* Oh. Hello, can I help you?

Wendell: Hi, Miss Beverly. I'm Wendell from the little store in Bixby. You stop in most times when you come up here.

Beverly: Oh yes, of course Wendell. I didn't recognize you in all your winter clothes and no apron on. How's your wife doing?

Wendell: She's fine, other than a little touch of rheumatism. Can I come in a minute?

Beverly: Sure. What can we do for you, Wendell? *(He enters, removes his coat and sits at the table.)*

Wendell: Got a cup of coffee?

Beverly: We do. The girls are just putting up the tree and some coffee would be good for all of us.

(Beverly goes to make the coffee and uncovers a plate with several kinds of Christmas cookies on it.)

Shonda: *(Walking over to Wendell.)* How long has your camp store been in business, Wendell?

Wendell: Well, my Dad had it for thirty years and I took over from him when I was about 30. So, I guess about 60 years.

Shonda: I remember a couple of Summer trips up here with Dad. You have quite the collection of live bait during fishing season.

Wendell: That we do. My wife's the one that catches most of it. She loves going to the creek and digging up the worms and crawdads. Gives me the creeps to tell you the truth. Never liked fishing.

Brenda: She is quite the outdoorswoman, apparently. *(Rolling her eyes.)*

(Beverly brings the cookies and sets them on the table. She sets some napkins next to the plate.)

Beverly: The coffee will be ready in a minute. Please have some cookies.

Shonda: *(Taking a cookie.)* So, what brings you up here to see us?

Wendell: Oh yeah, I almost forgot. Your husband Bill called. I figure he couldn't get you on your cell phone way up the mountain here.

Beverly: Bill tried to call? *(She goes to her purse and looks for her phone.)* You're right. No signal.

Wendell: He was late getting away from town, so don't worry about him. He is also bringing a surprise guest, so the girls will need to double up in the second bedroom so that your guest can have the other bedroom.

Brenda: Oh great. I get the snore queen.

Shonda: You only have to endure a little snoring. I have to smell your face cream all night. We may have to sleep with the window open a crack.

Brenda: Then expect to wake up with raccoons or squirrels in our beds. There are no screens on those windows, remember.

Shonda: That sounds fun. Racoons are furry and cuddly.

Beverly: This doesn't sound like Bill at all. I've asked him before to bring others along on our family trips and he always says, "No. It's family time." Why would he bring someone along, and at Christmas no less?

Wendell: Hey, thanks for the cookies. I need to hurry back down to the store. We're closing up soon for the night. The missus told me to hurry back before the snow gets bad.

Beverly: What about your coffee?

Wendell: No time. I will have to take a rain check. *(Wendell rises, puts his coat back on and exits.)*

Shonda: So, we will have a mystery guest. That's so odd. I wonder who it can be?

Brenda: My money is on an old army buddy of Dad's.

Beverly: Something is going on. I don't know what, but this is just so unlike Bill.

(Shonda walks over to the window and looks out.)

Shonda: I'll bet he's bringing some business colleague that is stuck here over the holidays.

Brenda: Oh rats, I wish I had guessed business guy. That was a good one, Shonda.

Shonda: Here comes his car now.

Beverly: Thank goodness, he made it up the mountain road.

Shonda: He has a woman with him, she looks like she is about our age, Brenda.

(Bill and Marcie enter.)

Beverly: *(Kissing Bill.)* You made it honey. So glad you are here. Were the roads bad?

Bill: It's getting slick out there, but we made it. Say hello to Marcie everyone.

Marcie: Hello all. *(She is carrying an overnight satchel and a large, artist's sketch pad.)*

Shonda: Nice to meet you. Are you into art?

Marcie: Oh yes, drawing is my thing. I figured the mountains might provide some inspiration.

(Brenda waves, but keeps decorating the tree.)

Beverly: Please come in. Set your stuff down anywhere. We will show you to your bedroom in a bit.

Marcie: Thanks for having me. I have always wanted to meet you.

Beverly: You have? How did you hear of us? It sounds like you have quite a story. Come on in and have a seat at the table. We were just about to have some coffee and cookies as a snack.

(Beverly gives Bill a look and leads the way to the table. She then goes over to the kitchen counter and retrieves the pot of coffee and cups.)

Bill: We can talk about everything later. I'm just glad we are all here together for the weekend. Looks like snowboard weather tomorrow.

Shonda: I can't wait!

Brenda: No broken bones for me. I will sit back and watch you daredevils come down the hill.

Shonda: So Marcie, tell us how you came to spend Christmas with us.

Beverly: Shonda, that sounded unwelcoming. We are glad you are here with us, Marcie. Welcome.

Marcie: Thank you. It is natural to have questions. I lost my Mom last month. I don't mean to barge into your family thing.

Beverly: I'm so sorry for your loss.

Marcie: It has been pretty rough. I've known Bill through Mom for most of my life. She worked at his company. He thought I might be lonely, so he took mercy on me. Don't I sound like a charity case?

Shonda: Not at all honey. We are going to have a great weekend. Come on. Let Brenda and I show you where you will sleep.

Marcie: Okay. That would be nice. I'd like to freshen up a bit.

Brenda: The room is right through here and the shared bath is across the hall. *(The three young ladies exit.)*

Beverly: Bill, that was either very nice of you or something more is going on.

Bill: Beverly, I would have talked this over with you– if I could have. Things happened rather quickly this afternoon. Then, your cell phone wasn't working. I called Wendell at the store to tell you I would be late. Did you stop at the store?

Beverly: No, but Wendell came up and told us the scoop just a few minutes ago. Who is this girl really?

Bill: Beverly, I don't want to keep this secret from you any longer. Marcie is my daughter.

Beverly: *(Pauses to let the news sink in.)* What are you saying?

Bill: I'm saying the girl in the other room is my daughter. Marcie's mother was a co-worker of mine a long time ago. She and I dated briefly not long before I met you. Then, she transferred to our Seattle office – to hide the pregnancy. For years, I didn't know that Gloria had a daughter. I sure didn't know that Marcie was my daughter. Gloria didn't want me to know. Long story short, about a year ago, the Seattle office closed. Gloria had no choice except to transfer back here or lose her job. She probably figured that so much time had passed, no one would suspect anything. Eventually, she told me the story.

Beverly: You've known this for a year and didn't tell me. Bill, you have a daughter with another woman and you didn't tell me?

Bill: *(Defensively.)* Not a year. She had been back a while before she told me. Gloria developed severe headaches and was diagnosed with a fast-developing brain cancer. She wanted Marcie and I to meet, so she brought her into the office. Slowly, Gloria told me the whole story. Since she and Marcie had very few living relatives on her side of the family, Gloria hoped that Marcie could meet all of us and eventually be accepted as part of our family. She just didn't want her daughter to be left alone.

Beverly: Wow. That's a lot to hear. That is a whole lot to process. *(Beverly crosses her arms.)*

Bill: And I don't expect you to instantly embrace the idea. Just let the God part of your heart lead you. This weekend, stay open and just stick your big toe in the water, so to speak.

Beverly: It bothers me that you brought her here, with our daughters to our place. And without telling us first. You didn't think to ask me?

Bill: I tried to ask you. It was the way things developed today. I didn't want to leave a depressed girl by herself on Christmas when we could so easily add one more plate at the table. My administrative assistant bought and wrapped a present for Marcie—so she will have something under the tree.

(The girls' voices can be heard coming back into the living room/ kitchen area.)

Beverly: We have a lot more to discuss.

Bill: How did it go?

Brenda: *(Smiling at the other two girls...)* It went fine. Marcie uses the same eye care products as Shonda, so she can't be all bad.

Marcie: They were very nice to show me around. I apologize for how last minute this turned out. It suddenly dawned on me that being alone this Christmas was going to be tough.

Beverly: Your Christmas will probably be tough either way, with company or without, but we are glad you came. It is so hard around the holidays when we are missing a loved one.

Brenda: Well, let's get the snacks and board games going and see if our newcomer can play Risk better than Dad.

Marcie: That's okay. I can watch you guys play.

Shonda: Nonsense. You can be my partner. It takes some people forever to play. The game is our excuse to tell stories and laugh.

(Everyone gathers around the table as Beverly and Brenda bring snacks over. Bill gets the game set up.)

Brenda: Tell us about Washington State. How did you like growing up on the other side of the Country?

Marcie: There were a lot of things I liked. The art scene around Seattle is so special. I have several artist friends there. I'm thinking of going back now that Mom has passed away. The only thing holding me here is my job. Although it is tough to get into commercial art, something tells me that going home to Seattle is the right move.

Shonda: Well, that's understandable. Did you have a special fella back there? Mr. Cool Artist Dude perhaps?

Marcie: Not really. My high school boyfriend and I were off and on during college, but I never really found that right guy. Just like my Mom, I guess.

Beverly: *(A little flustered.)* Do you have other relatives back in Seattle?

Shonda: Yeah, what about your Dad and his side of the family?

Marcie: That's complicated. My Mom was an only child. Grandpa died several years ago, heart attack. Grandma is still living, but she is in a place for Alzheimer's. She doesn't know anyone any more.

Shonda: And your Dad?

(Marcie gets choked up and runs out of the room.)

Brenda: Well, nice job Shonda. You made the new girl cry.

Bill: This is my fault. Girls, I have something to tell you.

Beverly: Are you sure? Now?

Bill: Yes. The secrets have gone on long enough. Marcie is my child. She grew up not knowing me and I didn't know about her until several months ago.

(Everyone is silent.)

Beverly: Well, go on. The cat's out of the bag now.

Bill: Marcie came into my life when her Mom returned to our office last February. Soon afterwards, Gloria was diagnosed with brain cancer. When that happened, Gloria decided to tell me why she left town in the first place. She was my girlfriend before I met your mother. Turns out, she got pregnant very soon after we met. Gloria didn't want to force me into some kind of relationship just to fit the circumstances. So, she took a transfer to Seattle.

Brenda: Hold it a second. You were having relations before you were married? Tsk. Tsk, Daddy. All those lectures to me about boys in high school...

Bill: Oh, I deserve that. You are right. Back then, I didn't know God and I certainly wasn't living according to His principles. All this is the result. The good news is that Marcie and I found each other at a time when she needed me most, needed all of us.

Shonda: Knock me over with a feather.

Brenda: Shut the barn door and milk the cow.

Beverly: Girls, we are from Fairfax, Virginia, not farm country.

Shonda: Thanks for the reality check Mom. Dad, this is going to take a little getting used to, but I think there is enough room in our family for one more.

Brenda: And enough love. She seems like a sweet girl.

Beverly: And enough cheeseball and crackers.

Bill: (*Sees Marcie standing in the doorway to the bedrooms.*) Oh Marcie. How much did you hear?

Marcie: Enough to know that you are planning to cut me in on the cheeseball and crackers.

(*Everyone gets up and group hugs Marcie. Eventually Beverly drifts away from the others and talks to the audience.*)

Beverly: We never know what curveballs life is going to throw at us. Love is always the right response. A long time ago, the world seemed so lost, desperately in need of a savior. Then, some humble shepherds heard angels sing. Next thing you know, the whole world found out about a baby born in Bethlehem. Our family has enough love to include one more person for Christmas. How about yours? Is there someone in your circle of acquaintance who needs a friend? Why not open up your world this Christmas and extend the savior's love. You might find so much more love than you expect. Merry Christmas, everyone!

Cast: Merry Christmas!

5

Grandma Louise's Christmas Miracle

Written by David L. Winters

Cast

Cynthia   Mother of Paris and Judith, newswoman

Paris   Younger daughter of Cynthia

Judith   Older daughter of Cynthia

Grandma Louise   Mother of Cynthia, Outspoken

Jack   Cynthia's brother, movie cameraman

Santa   St. Nick

Scene 1

(Setting: Well-lit living room with Christmas tree and fireplace.)

(Paris and Judith enter and sit staring at presents.)

Judith: Paris, what do you think you are getting for Christmas?

Paris: *(Very excited.)* I don't know. I sure hope it is a new iPad or laptop and I can't live without a new Dr. Who T-shirt and there are so many other things I want.

Judith: Let me give you a little older sister advice. It is best to pray and hope, but be open to whatever comes your way. That way you won't be too disappointed.

Paris: Oh Judith, I know. I know. I know. But there are so many games for the iPad. All my friends have them already. A nice big fat gift card to the Apple store is just what the doctor ordered. Think of the fun sleepovers I could have. Oh, if Mom asks, I want the iPad for school work too.

Judith: Save that kind of talk for Mom. I know you, Paris.

(Cynthia and Grandma Louise enter.)

Cynthia: That is so nice of Jack to load the dishwasher for us. He is a nice brother after all.

Grandma: He is a wonderful boy. Always has been. And a movie cameraman too.

Judith: Grandma, what do you want Santa to bring you for Christmas?

Grandma: Judith, old Saint Nick and me have an understanding. As long as he don't bring me any more wrinkles, rheumatism or regrets, everything else is gravy.

Cynthia: And no more fancy bathrobes.

Grandma: Can you blame me? I got bathrobes seven Christmases in a row. You people think all I do is sit around in my robe all day.

Paris: You do get up kind of late.

Cynthia: And get dressed kind of late.

Judith: And look great in fancy nightgowns.

Grandma: Santa knows what I want, but I don't think he has one of those in his big red bag.

Paris: As long as he has a laptop or iPad in his bag for me, I'm going to be happy.

Cynthia: I tell you one thing. If you do get a new electronic device you better plan right now to have some limits on it. Screen time limits aren't going away for anyone in this house. We won't be sitting around ignoring each other and going blind staring at our computer screens all day and night.

Paris: Absolutely, Mom. You are the boss.

Grandma: If you ask me, the whole internet is of the devil.

(Jack enters.)

Cynthia: Jack, thank you so much for getting the dishes in the dishwasher.

Jack: No worries, sister. It's good for a bachelor like me to remember how to clean up a kitchen. I eat out almost every meal, except when I'm microwaving.

Judith: Uncle Jack, why aren't you married? You seem like a pretty good catch.

Paris: I would marry you if we weren't related.

Cynthia: Girls, it is a little rude to interrogate your uncle, particularly on Christmas Eve.

Jack: I'm not dead yet girls. I may get married eventually. Just needed to be free to look around the world and see what's out there.

Grandma: And that you have done. Who knew being a cameraman for the movies would take you to India and China?

Cynthia: It's ironic. I got into broadcast news to travel and cover all sorts of news events. I end up as a local anchorwoman and my brother travels the world with movie stars.

Judith: Beloved local anchorwoman...

Jack: To be honest, the actors tend to stick with other actors and the technical people tend to hang out with each other. But I have enjoyed the travel. Seeing the way other people live has been fascinating. I'll bet Mom could tell us some stories about her mission trips.

Judith: Grandma Louise, tell us one of your stories from the mission field. We love hearing about your adventures.

Grandma: Cynthia, can you get me a cup of coffee? Might need to wet my whistle along the way.

Cynthia: Sure, Mom. You get started and I will retrieve the coffee. Anyone else need anything?

(No one else speaks up, so Cynthia retreats to the kitchen.)

Grandma: Well, let's see. Oh, I know one I've never told you. It happened right at Christmas in the interior of Africa. I couldn't have been more than twenty-two-years-old at the time. Your grandfather and I were on assignment from our church headquarters. As volunteer, short-termers, we were flown into remote villages. Our mission centered around verifying that church money was spent correctly.

Paris: So, you were kind of like the missionary money police?

Grandma: More like the mission auditors. We received print-outs about everything that was paid for to go to each location. Then, we would travel there, inspect the equipment or building or whatever, and fly out the next day.

Cynthia: *(Setting down the coffee cup next to her.)* I'll bet the locals were glad to see you.

Grandma: They treated us like kings and queens. In their mind, we represented all the love that sent them a new well, or twenty chickens or whatever. This village I'm talking about was called Martitobi. Our denomination had recently paid for an orphanage building, a central meeting house, school desks and chairs. In addition, there was supposed to be all kinds of school supplies, including paper, pens, textbooks and the like. Mason was the name of our pilot. As we flew over the jungle from the nearest city, Dad and I loved looking over the beautiful, green landscape. We were on our way to Martitobi during the rainy season; everything in this part of Africa turned lush. In an instant, all of us heard something hit the plane.

Paris: Were you scared?

Judith: What was it? What hit the plane?

Grandma: No, I wasn't too scared. Before our trip, your grandfather and I had already agreed that we were willing to risk our lives for the Gospel. It was that important to us. So, we felt calm in our hearts. In my head though, I did not want the plane to go down in the jungle. Hostile military forces roamed the countryside, looking for people like us to rob and even physically harm.

Judith: So, what happened? Did you get captured by hostile forces?

Grandma: Mason told us that whatever hit the plane must have damaged the fuel tank. His gauge went from almost full to almost empty just like that.

So, we all needed to pray for an appropriate place to land and get it repaired. We also were going to need more fuel.

Cynthia: Oh goodness, Mom. How did I miss this story all my life?

Grandma: I probably told you about it during your teenage years when you didn't listen to anything I said. Anyway, God provided a tiny airstrip. Mason safely set the plane down and did a bush fix on the fuel tank. The little landing strip had no fuel, but they did have a telephone nearby. So, Mason called and arranged for more fuel to be delivered in large drums, enough to get us to Martitoba and back to the Capital city. Our adventure was not over though. When we got to Martitoba, the holy man there was very suspicious of us and of the new school that towered over one end of the town. Picture a town with a bunch of grass huts and then a cinderblock school, a cinderblock orphanage and associated livestock? The holy man thought someone was trying to usurp his power. And we represented that someone.

Cynthia: What did he do to get his point across?

Grandma: He gathered some men to play the drums and dance around, putting curses on father and myself. While we didn't worry about his vain carrying on, the townspeople were very scared of him.

Judith: Was he like a witch doctor?

Grandma: Sort of. He had a scepter made out of reeds, with various brightly-colored feathers and beads hanging from it. He would dance around and shake the scepter in our direction. One night when most of the town was gone to a neighboring village for a big celebration, the holy man, as they called him, came to visit father and I.

Judith: Just the three of you? What did he want?

Grandma: He told us that he didn't believe in our God, but he did believe in Santa Claus. Can you imagine us, two westerners hearing this holy man affirm his belief in Santa, but not God? Father asked him what God could do to prove His love for the village and him in particular. He said he would only believe if Santa came to the village with presents for everyone.

Judith: Grandma Louise, that is crazy. This witch doctor in the middle Africa wanted God to prove himself by sending Santa to the village with presents?

Paris: I'm liking the way this witch doctor thinks.

Grandma: Well, needless to say, Father and I had no idea how God was going to work this out, but Father told Him that we would pray. It was up to God because we had no way to summon a Santa or to get presents for everyone so far out in the wilderness. To further complicate things, our plane wasn't coming back for another five days. As far as we knew, God was on his own if this prayer request was to be answered.

(Paris walks over to the window and looks out.)

Paris: So, the witch doctor didn't get his miracle, did he?

Cynthia: Paris, I'm surprised at you. Why so skeptical?

Paris: I've prayed for Daddy to come home to us since I was a little girl, but he hasn't shown up.

Judith: Paris, you know he can't. Daddy is in heaven.

Paris: That's what the Navy said, but they never found his body. His plane was found, but they never found his body. Did they mamma?

Cynthia: *(Hugging Paris.)* No dear, they never found his body. It isn't wrong to hope, but we also have to go on with our lives. God has sustained us in so many ways, even though we don't know the truth.

Grandma: Well, back to my story. Father must have stayed awake half the night praying. I prayed even longer. Both of us knew how much good it could do if the holy man's prayer got answered. In the morning, Father was still sleeping on his side of the clay hut. Usually, he would have been up running around by then. I called to him and he roused. Then we both heard loud voices coming from the other side of the camp. The noise got louder and louder until we feared a full-scale riot was breaking out.

Judith: What in the world was happening?

Paris: Did Santa Claus miraculously appear?

Grandma: Well, Father and I got up and went outside. In the middle of all the villagers sat a man who looked a lot like Santa Claus sitting on a motor-cycle.

Jack: Goodness gracious. How come you never told me this story before?

Grandma Louise: You've never shown the least interest in my missionary stories.

Judith: Well, did he have presents for everyone in the village?

Grandma: Father and I were Methodists, but as it turns out, this guy was a Baptist missionary. On his back was a huge bag with all kinds of small gifts, including pens, writing paper, books, sealed candies and a shortwave radio for the holy man *(or leader of the village.)*

Paris: So, God did exactly what the witch doctor wanted?

Cynthia: It sounds like God was willing to go to great lengths to show his love for the whole village.

Paris: *(Wistfully)* So, they got their Christmas miracle.

Judith: I know what you are thinking. Why can't you have your Christmas miracle? Why can't Dad suddenly come back from the grave and spend Christmas with us.

Cynthia: Oh Paris honey, I know how much you want

to see your Daddy. This may be impossible though. Instead of telling God the exact miracle He has to give us, let's pray for His best miracle for us this Christmas. Would that be okay?

Paris: Okay.

Cynthia: Lord, you know how much Paris misses her Dad. Please send us your very best miracle this Christmas. We trust you and leave it your hands. Amen. Mom, was there more to your story.

Grandma: Just the best part. The arrival of Santa led to a revival service. Daddy and the Baptist guy both preached. I taught them a couple of songs. Before it was all over, several people gave their hearts to Jesus. By the time our plane came back for us, neither Daddy nor I wanted to leave. But, Mom and my college schoolwork was waiting for us. So, we took that same little plane back to the main city, rejoicing all the way.

Cynthia: That was a great story, Mom. Let's all turn in now, so that we can get up early and exchange presents before breakfast and church.

Jack: Sounds good to me. Paris, why don't we prepare some milk and cookies to leave out for Santa Claus?

Paris: Okay. Come on to the kitchen. (*They both exit and everyone else goes to their bedrooms.*)

(*Scene goes dark.*)

Scene 2

(Living Room is now filled with presents, particularly under the tree. St. Nick is eating cookies left for him on the mantle.)

Paris: *(Enters.)* Aha! I caught you. What are you doing?

St. Nick: Oh, hi there, young lady. Just having one of the cookies you left out for me.

Paris: Is it really you? I thought you didn't exist.

St. Nick: Gee Whiz. Not that again. Why do people have so much trouble believing in old St. Nick? I really have to get a better publicist.

Paris: If you are St. Nick, you would know what I really, really wanted for Christmas.

St. Nick: iPad and don't skimp on the video games.

Paris: It is you!

Judith: *(Enters.)* I thought I heard voices. Hey. Who are you and what are you doing in our house on Christmas Eve.

St. Nick: Here we go again. Well, I brought a bunch of presents. Put them under the tree. Woofed down a couple of cookies. By the way, I loved the Angel Mysteries. The apricot was exquisite.

Paris: My Grandma Louise makes those. They are delicious!

Judith: Who are you really? Before I call the cops...

St Nick: Don't be rash. They get hundreds of calls about me. Be prepared to take a breathalyzer test.

Paris: Don't call the police on Santa.

Judith: *(Yells.)* Mom, Grandma, Uncle Jack, there is some weirdo in our living room.

(Cynthia, Grandma Louise and Uncle Jack enter. Jack's carrying a baseball bat.)

Jack: Stand back. I can handle this. *(Threatens Santa with the bat.)*

Paris: *(Jumps in front of St. Nick.)* Don't hit Santa.

Cynthia: I see you've met our St. Nick.

Grandma: Goodness gracious. You about gave me a heart attack. Cynthia, who is this man?

Cynthia: St. Nick. Let's all sit down. He has a story to tell also.

(Everyone sits down.)

St Nick: Well. I guess I should say what I came to tell you. Paris, Judith, I was a friend of your father in Afghanistan.

Judith: You were?

St Nick: Yes. We knew each other for about five months. Your father had pictures of both of you and Cynthia too. He kept them on the inside of his foot locker. Whenever he lifted the top to get anything at all, there you were, smiling back at him. He loved you with all of his heart. Paris, you were sitting on a tricycle and Judith, you were standing behind her in a green dress.

Paris: I know that picture.

St Nick: Your Dad was so loved and cared about by the other guys in our unit. He had a great sense of humor and used to play jokes on the other guys. But if anyone needed help, he tried to provide it. Just a great guy.

Paris: Did he die?

St Nick: Yes, Paris. I'm afraid he did. Your father was an explosives expert. We were working to clear out some caves. He went down a path and into a cave. I was watching for the enemy to show up. Suddenly, there was a loud blast from the direction that your Dad went. The Taliban set a boobytrap, hoping to kill several of us. Thanks to your Dad's bravery, he was the only one that died. When the explosion went off, the whole side of the mountain came down. We tried to move in and recover his body, but there was no way with the number of enemy snipers and the extent of the cave in. So, the Army eventually labelled him Missing in Action.

Paris: So he died?

St Nick: I'm afraid so.

Judith: And you are 100 percent sure?

St Nick: Yes. I know this wasn't the Christmas miracle

you were hoping for. For the last several years, I was stuck in an Army hospital, recovering from the effects of an ambush. During that time, there was this overwhelming feeling that when I recovered, I was supposed to find you and tell you the story.

Cynthia   When St. Nick and I talked a few days ago, I asked him to come here and tell you the story in person.

St Nick: And I was happy to do it. You all deserved to hear the truth from someone who was there.

Paris: *(Walking up to St. Nick)* Thank you. Thank you for telling us. It wasn't the miracle I wanted, but I feel better knowing the real truth.

Judith: Me too.

St Nick: Well, enjoy the presents. Thanks for the tea and cookies. (Cynthia escorts him to the door.)

Jack: Well, let's dig into those presents.

Grandma: Me first. (She opens her first gift and it is a frilly bathrobe.) Another bathrobe!

David L. Winters (1959-) is an author, speaker and humorist. He was born in Ohio and now resides in the Washington, D.C. suburbs. After 35 years in Government Service, he now writes and speaks full-time. His first non-fiction work, *Sabbatical of the Mind: The Journey from Anxiety to Peace* won several awards. He also wrote The Driver Series, a fiction trilogy. *Driver Confessional* relates the story of a Christian ride-share driver who stumbles onto a murder and ends up running for his life from the Russian mafia.

Made in the USA
Monee, IL
08 August 2023

40687323R00050